"Leadership is the art of accomplishing more than the science of management says is possible."

"A good leader surrounds himself with people who complement his skills. Only an honest and fair assessment of your abilities will allow this to happen."

The Powell Principles

24 Lessons from Colin Powell, a Legendary Leader

OREN HARARI

McGraw-Hill

New York Chicago San Francisco Lisbon
London Madrid Mexico City Milan New Delhi
San Juan Seoul Singapore Sydney Toronto

The McGraw·Hill Companies

Copyright © 2003 by Oren Harari. Printed in the United States of America. Except as permitted under the United States Copyright Act of 1976, no part of this publication may be reproduced or distributed in any form or by any means, or stored in a data base or retrieval system, without the prior written permission of the publisher.

1 2 3 4 5 6 7 8 9 0   DOC/DOC   0 6 5 4 3 2

ISBN 0-07-141109-7

Production services provided by CWL Publishing Enterprises, Madison, WI, www.cwlpub.com.

 This book is printed on recycled, acid-free paper containing a minimum of 50% recycled, de-inked fiber.

McGraw-Hill books are available at special quantity discounts to use as premiums and sales promotions, or for use in corporate training programs. For more information, please write to the Director of Special Sales, Professional Publishing, McGraw-Hill, Two Penn Plaza, New York, NY 10121-2298. Or contact your local bookstore.

The Powell Principles is in no way authorized or endorsed by or affiliated with General Colin Powell.

To order
The Powell Principles
call 1-800-842-3075

Contents

☑ *The Powell Principles*

---

*C*olin Powell has enjoyed a truly extraordinary career. His is a child-of-immigrants' tale, embodying strong values, hard work, discipline, exceptional standards, and high integrity. Today, Powell is viewed as a hero by Americans of all stripes—and also by non-Americans. He's also one of the strongest and most able leaders that this country has known.

In September 1993, Powell retired from the military with full honors. During his military career, he not only personally command-ed everything from small platoons to enormous units, but was also a key player in leading American forces through wars, regional battles, and humanitarian efforts.

His career after his "retirement" has been equally impressive, ranging from public speaking to serving on the boards of many major corporations, to chairing the nonprofit America's Promise foundation—and culminating in his January 2001 appointment as Secretary of State in the Bush administration.

In studying Powell and his philosophy, it is clear that he espous-es—and far more difficult, *practices*—many of the mental maps, deci-sion-making habits, and other behaviors that characterize effective leadership. In the wake of the September 11th terrorist attacks, Powell quickly emerged as one of the key players in our country's effort to prevent future terrorism in any form. And although Powell was at the epicenter of waging a new brand of war in a crisis situation, you wouldn't have known it to look at him. He appeared calm, assured, dignified, and prepared—just as he had looked under various microscopes for the preceding several decades. The rules had changed, and dramatically, but—at least as far as the public would see—Powell had not. His leadership compass remained true.

The following lessons in leadership outline the Powell Principles—the practical, mission- and people-based leadership that Powell has practiced throughout his career and that has translated into performance excellence and competitive success.

Whether you run a small family business, a large corporation, or a National Guard unit, these lessons will help you grow your leadership talents: they offer wisdom that you can apply to your own situation.

"Management is easy. Leadership is motivating people, turning people on, getting 110% out of a personal relationship."

☑ *Promote a clash of ideas*

*I*n today's world, Powell argues, ideas matter. Ideas build up, or bring down, empires. To be successful, leaders must consciously work to stay in touch with the best ideas of the people they lead. Hasn't the organization invested considerable resources in the recruitment and training of these good people? Well, then, the organization ought to get the benefit of that investment. Its leaders ought to be on the lookout, constantly, for great ideas.

This is not just a process of installing a relief valve, and it's not just a way to harvest ideas. It's also a process of involving people in— and making them take responsibility for—the shaping of their ideas. Yes, by opening up the pipeline, the leader may well unleash a flood of interesting and provocative insights. But the ultimate goal is to inspire people in the organization not just to voice problems, but also to figure out ways to solve problems.

When it comes down to it, the physical or financial assets of a company are far less important to its success than its idea base. The key question is, how many fresh, innovative, shared, actionable ideas are bubbling away in the corporate cauldron? And just as important, how accessible are those ideas?

In all too many companies, important decisions are made behind closed doors, with surprisingly limited input from below. Vital information is hoarded in specific levels in the management hierarchy, or within functional "silos." In many cases, the organization is so walled off that the best people in Department A effectively have no idea of what their skilled counterparts in Department B are doing.

Small wonder, then, that so many organizations fail to adapt. Without clashing opinions, organizations stagnate. The organization needs to use noisy systems and creative clashes to pump up its own pulse—and, of course, its leaders need to keep a finger squarely on that pulse. Here are three techniques you can use to encourage a clash of ideas:

Encourage a noisy system: This effort has to go far beyond the confines of the traditional "suggestion box." An organization's leader must use every means to reach out, encouraging a diversity of opinion and what Powell calls a "clash of ideas."

Look for great ideas ... wherever they come from: Encourage communication from every direction, and never let rank or hierarchy get in the way. Smoke out the opinions of those closest to the front lines. Invite "outsiders" into the discussion.

Speed communication through technology: Harness the power of the new technologies in order to ensure that everyone is included. Invest the necessary resources, and create the psychological climate in which information flowing freely over networks is seen as a resource, rather than a threat.

"I want to hear all the rough edges of all arguments. I don't want to concur things to death and coordinate things to death so I get a round pebble instead of a stone that has edges on it. I want to hear from you."

☑ *Be prepared to piss people off*

*C*olin Powell is above all a *gentleman*. He's unfailingly polite—the very embodiment of civility. He's not interested in intimidating people. Why? Because, aside from being a gentleman, he also is convinced that frightened people don't take initiative or responsibility, and that their organizations suffer as a result. And yet, he's perfectly prepared to make people angry—even *really* angry—in pursuit of organizational excellence. His explanation for this seeming inconsistency is pithy: "Being responsible sometimes means pissing people off."

Leadership can't be a popularity contest. Trying not to offend anyone, or trying to get everyone to like you, are signposts on the road to mediocrity. Leaders who are afraid to get people angry are likely to waver and procrastinate when it comes to making tough choices. Leaders who care more about being *liked* than being *effective* are unlikely to confront the people who need confronting. They are unlikely to offer differential rewards based on performance. In short, they won't challenge the status quo. And inevitably, by so doing, they hurt both their own credibility and their organization's performance.

A good leader ensures that the right people are getting pissed off, and the wrong people aren't. Phrasing it a little more positively, Powell believes that *good leaders focus ceaselessly on making sure that their best people are the most satisfied.*

Leaders should clarify, exhort, and push. They should confront employees, peers, or partners whose performance is sub-par (or no longer appropriate for a changed business context). By failing in those responsibilities, managers are putting their organization in harm's way. Here are several things you can do to assure that you're sparking the changes—in direction, and in urgency—that are absolutely necessary for your organization's revitalization and success:

Make performance and change top organizational priorities: Encourage experimentation and innovative initiatives to replace "the old way." Provide people with tools, technologies, and training to build their skill sets and enhance their sense of personal responsibility.

Reward your best performers, and get rid of non-performers: Remember that this is not a zero-sum game, and that there's plenty for everyone, as long as performance counts. But don't take the easy, "across the board" way out. And unload people who can't or won't perform.

Encourage creative disruption: Random hostilities are not what the organization needs, but if nobody's pissed off, maybe you're not pushing hard enough.

"Being responsible sometimes means pissing people off."

☑ *Establish trust*

---

*T*rust is essential for influence and credibility. How do you build trust? *By demonstrating the key attributes and personal traits that are likely to build people's confidence in you.* According to Powell, these attributes are competence, character, courage, loyalty, and confidence.

We are inclined to trust those people who have relevant knowledge and experience, and can keep the organization whole and healthy. This is **competence**, and it's a prerequisite of leadership. But competence also means the ability to learn on a continuing basis, to build harmonious and collaborative relationships, and to fire up peoples' curiosity.

We also tend to trust people with **character**, *people who stand for something*—a value, an ideal, a cause, a mission. They show a coherent pattern of behavior and decisions that clarify and reinforce in the eyes of all around them what the leader stands for. In Powell's words, they "figure out what is crucial," and then they "stay focused on it."

Courage is a close corollary to character. As a career military man, Powell rates this trait very highly. In any context, though, leaders should ask themselves the "courage question": *Even if I'm doing things right, am I doing the right thing?* Am I standing for that right thing even in the face of adversity?

Loyalty is a fourth key building block to trust. For Powell, loyalty is a signpost that points three ways: up, down, and sideways. He also believes that the leader has to take the initiative by demonstrating loyalty to his troops.

Finally, there's **confidence**. This raises the issue of "ego." No one gets and holds a leadership position without a healthy dose of ego. And ego—combined with commitment to mission—is what builds confidence. For Powell, confidence is an issue of certainty and resolve: certainty in the mission you are trying to accomplish, and resolve in doing whatever it takes tactically to achieve your goals.

Here are three tactics that can help build the trust of those you lead:

Never underestimate the "Trust Factor": The Powell Principles are about building trust. Trust comes from exhibiting many key traits, including competence, character, courage, loyalty, confidence, self-lessness, sacrifice, and empathy.

Encourage communication: A leader has a responsibility to be available to his troops. Giving them an easy opportunity to speak their piece, without fear of retribution, builds trust throughout the entire organization.

Be a servant leader: Help people to accomplish the goals that emanate from the vision. Give them the tools they need, and turn them loose.

"Why would you follow somebody around a corner? Or up the hill? Or into a dark room? The reason is trust."

☐ Talk a good game

☑ *Walk the talk*

---

*F*ew things matter more to Powell than personal integrity. People with integrity clearly "stand for" something bigger than themselves—a purpose, or a core set of values and ideals—and their actions honestly reflect these convictions. There is a coherence in their decisions and behaviors that reflects their ideals. They are persistent and consistent in how they express their values, and therefore are tenacious in pursuing their purpose. As a leader, integrity means practicing what you preach. Leaders who talk a good game but do not lead by example will not be respected. They must live by the traits they espouse.

A person with a weak sense of integrity is likely to make expedient decisions. He or she is likely to be focused keenly on organizational politics, or directed primarily by self-interest, or driven by what he or she thinks the organization wants to hear. In other words, a lack of integrity is not simply an ethical concern; it also poses a clear threat to the effective functioning of the organization.

If you want your organization to conduct itself in an ethical way—with integrity—then you need to demonstrate personal integrity, setting high standards of conduct for your employees. If your employees don't see this at the highest level of the organization, they won't be inspired to meet the standards you've set. Anytime there is a gap between what a leader says and what that leader does, the credibility of that individual will suffer, and sometimes the cost will be too much for the leader (and the organization) to bear. How do you walk the talk? Consider these three ideas:

7

Practice empathy and selflessness: Understand the hardships and sacrifices of those under you... and be prepared to share these hardships yourself.

Curiosity is a key leadership ingredient: The best leaders arouse curiosity. They are interesting and are able to inspire others to act. Boring people stifle curiosity, and drive away potential followers.

Use influence, not authority: People will always be more inclined to follow a leader whose mantra is "do as I do" rather than "do as I say." Influence accomplishes as much as—if not more than authority ... and it leaves a better residue.

"You can issue all the memos and give all the motivational speeches you want, but if the rest of the people in your organization don't see you putting forth your best effort every single day, they won't either."

☐ **Pick people with resumes**

☑ *Pick the right people*

---

*H*ow do you accomplish great things? Only by attracting the best people, according to Colin Powell. As many savvy executives have discovered, people aren't just a piece of the puzzle, they are the puzzle. Or more accurately, they're the solution to the puzzle.

The best people will develop the best ideas and the most effective follow-ups. They will develop the right technology, and the optimal application for it. They will figure out how to use available resources to connect with each other to develop the most exciting products, the most extraordinary cost reductions, the most dazzling customer services, the most lucrative niches, and the most promising investment opportunities. They'll help you define and attain your mission in ways you couldn't have dreamed of on your own.

Powell advises us to hire, place, and promote talented individuals with the following qualities: intelligence and judgment, a capacity to anticipate, loyalty, integrity, a high energy drive, a balanced ego and the drive to get things done.

This may sound like so much common sense. But in the heat of battle, it's all too easy to put undue emphasis on a plan (either its development or execution). And it's all too easy to forget that the stewardship of people is a *strategic* priority.

When you dig down into how organizations *actually assess* the talents of potential recruits, you find that in many cases, very different screens are put into place. What *actually* happens, more often than not, is that the human-resources staff focuses on attributes like length of resume, number of degrees, and previous job titles.

Powell's favorite attributes present none of these advantages. They are hard to infer from a resume. Of course, Powell would never reject individuals who possess specialized skills and experience, especially when today's crisis calls for those specific skills. He *would* insist, though, that in today's chaotic environments, other talents are likely to prove just as important over the long run. Here are three techniques you can use to pick the right people:

Hire talent and values, not just resumes: Resumes, by definition, describe past performance. They don't begin to indicate how someone will fare in your organization.

Seek value alignment: Don't hire or promote anyone who does not share the same values that drive your organization. Even a talented individual will find it hard to contribute to your mission if their values are not in synch with your own.

Hire people who compensate for your own weaknesses: Don't let your ego get in the way. Hire people you consider good enough to succeed you, should the situation warrant it. Strong leaders are not afraid to surround themselves with people better than themselves.

"You give me the right people, and I don't much care what organization you give me. Good things will happen. Give me the wrong people, and it doesn't matter what you do with the organization. Bad things will happen."

☐ Lecture

☑ *Listen*

---

*I*n a conversation with Powell, you are likely to be struck by how intently he listens. In fact, he seems more inclined to listen than be listened to.

This reflects Powell's determination to learn whatever he can, wherever he can. But it is also another example of Powell modeling the behavior that he believes will foster better communication. Good listening begets good listening. Ideas get exchanged faster and more reliably.

Good listening also makes it far easier to deliver bad news. When Powell visited Africa for the first time in June 2001, he impressed African leaders with his obvious determination to hear and understand what they were saying. His responses to their concerns—especially regarding the devastation that the AIDS virus was causing on their continent—were seen as clear evidence that he had heard and understood them.

The American press corps expressed surprise at Powell's remarkable display of candor. The African leaders, for their part, indicated that they would take the American's tough words to heart. Clearly, they heard Powell's message because it was part of a dialogue—an exchange of ideas. If he had simply attempted to *lecture* them, he (and his ideas) would have gotten nowhere.

When managers ascend the corporate hierarchy, they sometimes become afflicted with a curious problem: their ears get smaller and their mouths get bigger. Perversely, the more they say without hearing, the less likely they are to be heard. Leaders who *shut up and lis-*

ten not only learn a lot, but carve out an environment where others are willing to listen to them. Encouraging communication at all levels of the organization—and *listening* to the dialogue that results—raises the bar on individual and group performance. Here are three ways to show that you're listening:

Use every means to encourage communication: Sidestep bureaucracy and rank to smoke out the opinions of those closest to the front lines. Invite "outsiders" into the discussion to get the benefit of their insights.

Maintain one pure line of communication: Find people you trust and give them a way to provide you with feedback. This guarantees that the information you need won't get "managed" by some well-meaning staffer. (It also means that you must be ready to hear criti- cisms without any sugarcoating.)

Use symbols to encourage communication: The higher one goes up in the hierarchy, the harder one has to work to stay in touch with real people and real data. Use symbolism (like round tables, no dress code, etc.) to reinforce your availability.

"In the military, when you become a four-star general, people will do anything you even suggest you want .... I had to work at breaking down that deference to hear from my people."

☐ Stick to the big picture

☑ *Be vigilant in details*

---

*T*he Powell Principles are about carving out a clear mission, and then pursuing its objectives decisively. But it's also about mastering the details before you launch a campaign. There are lots of reasons to do so. First of all, the details will absolutely change the way you think about your options. Second, once you've settled on your option, mastery of the details leads to better execution and greater unit cohesion. And, not least important, the leader who has clearly mastered the details inspires confidence.

This is true not only up the organizational ladder, but also down that ladder. As Chairman of the Joint Chiefs of Staff, Powell once observed that "checking small things achieves two purposes. It reveals to the commander the real state of readiness in contrast to a surface appearance of readiness. And a general's attention to detail lets the soldier far down the chain know that his link is as vital as the one that precedes or follows."[1]

Senior executives are tugged in a thousand directions at once. "Big Picture" issues tend to overwhelm the details. (And indeed, we would fault the executive who neglected the Big Picture in favor of minutiae.) But the difficult fact remains that the Big Picture is made up of hundreds or thousands of details. A balance needs to be struck. Unfortunately, many leaders fail to strike it. They act based on an inadequate understanding of competitors' movements prior to a major strategic move, insufficient awareness of market realities prior to a product launch, or naive assumptions about what it'll take to integrate new systems and old cultures ... and so on, and so on. If you are not the master of the details, you can't be the master of the Big Picture.

It's *details*—in the form of timely and relevant data, information, knowledge—that minimize the risk of "haphazard," flaky, or just plain wrong policy decisions. The details won't by themselves generate the best solution or course of action, but paying attention to the details *will* increase the likelihood of sound analyses and creative insights. To make sure that details are getting enough attention in your organization, consider the following:

Master the details, then execute: Sound strategy requires sound execution. Even the best ideas are useless if they cannot be implemented; therefore, the details—grubby as they often are—will dictate the best course of action.

Stay in touch with the little things: As Powell says, "If you are going to achieve excellence in big things, you develop the habit in little matters." Ultimately, it may be attention to the small matters that may translate into a key victory. Don't lose touch—especially as you ascend the hierarchy.

Avoid "analysis paralysis": Attending to the fine points is not a license to micro-manage, hide from a decision, or delay.

"If you are going to achieve excellence in big things, you develop the habit in little matters. Excellence is not an exception, it is a prevailing attitude."

[1] Powell, Colin, with Joseph E. Persico, *My American Journey* (New York: Random House, 1995), p. 446.

☐ Let sleeping dogs lie

☑ *Be a disorganizer*

---

*O*ne reason why Colin Powell is an effective leader is that he is not easily misled by superficial analyses, surface truths, or "spin." This is a trait shared by good leaders across the board. They're experienced. They're hard to snow, snooker, or hoodwink. They know that the best paint job can be used to hide nasty things beneath the surface.

At the same time, they're hard to stampede. They've seen lots of dire predictions turn out to be Chicken Little warnings: The sky is falling! Very often, as it turns out, the sky isn't falling.

One way effective leaders guard against surprises, as Powell suggests, is through a more or less relentless process of digging and probing, combined with a clear and unblinking eye. If they dig and find a mess, well, they acknowledge that it's a mess and they take steps to clean it up. If they dig and find a hidden diamond, they celebrate—and then, of course, they keep digging.

Complacency is an organizational virus. Left unchecked, it gradually immobilizes people. And when it morphs into more deadly strains, like delusion or arrogance, then the hard fall is probably just around the corner. Effective leaders nip complacency in the bud and feel great urgency about doing so.

How is this accomplished? Powell has already given us a good answer: "Keep looking below surface appearances." Effective leaders *find the truth* and *face the truth*. They use the truth to make decisions that will move their organizations forward.

The job of the leader is not to be the chief organizer, but the chief disorganizer. A disorganizer is someone who continually picks at and harasses the routine of the organization. A disorganizer lifts up the covers, looks under the bed, and runs a finger along the tops of the bookcases, all so that he or she can pose and begin to answer the key question: *What are we doing, right or wrong, and how can it be improved?* To be a disorganizer, adopt the following Powell rules:

Look below the surface: Never stop doubting and challenging habits and conventional wisdom. Always look for alternate and better paths. Be the organization's primary agent for change.

Fight complacency: In today's world, contentment with the status quo is dangerous. Lead with a healthy dose of skepticism.

Dig, dig, and dig some more: An open-door policy is a good thing. But this alone won't get you to the truth below the surface. It is the leader's responsibility to constantly probe below the surface.

"Keep looking below surface appearances. Don't shrink from doing so just because you might not like what you find."

☑ *Check your ego at the door*

*A*s managers, much of *who we are* is wrapped up in *what we do*. We carefully create the status quo … and then we become prisoners of it. Our self-esteem, our career histories, our enterprise infrastructures, our technologies, our cultures and traditions, our skill sets, our views of competitors, customers, and partners—all combine to make us who we are, at least in the workplace. This is perfectly understandable. After all, humans are creatures of habit. Habits help us set limits on choice-making. Habits make us easier to work with. Habits serve us well.

The problem arises when the habits that define us focus primarily on the *past*. It's gratifying (and again, human) to want to dwell on the marketplace of yesterday, where we fought good battles and enjoyed great victories. It's tempting to see the marketplace of today—and tomorrow—as being very much like the marketplace of the past.

Unfortunately, it can't be and it won't be. Effective leaders, therefore, don't cling to familiar turfs. They don't let their egos distort the organizational agenda. They ferret out clues as to what tomorrow may look like. They use this information to set a new course and help others adjust their circumstances—both the individual and the corporate status quo—to reflect *tomorrow's* conditions.

Companies tend to turn a blind eye toward a changing environment for the same reason as individuals. Both companies and individuals invest in the status quo. They build up their enemies, and then they become dependent on those enemies. The health of their egos becomes linked, in a perverse way, with the health of their enemies.

In such circumstances, expert and energetic leadership is needed. Great leaders in business and government continually press for new "positions." They do so not just in times of crisis—when it's relatively easy to get most people to check their egos at the door—but also when things seem to be motoring along just fine. They find ways to share their own sense of urgency. Here are some ways to ensure that your ego doesn't interfere with your work:

Don't become a prisoner of your position: Leaders who cling to their established positions and standard operating procedures will place their enterprises in jeopardy.

Change before you are forced to change: Great leaders take a deep breath, walk right up to Change, and shake its hand. They check their egos and try on a new self-image. It's always less painful to change yourself than to have change forced upon you.

Reinvent your job before it's too late: When managers lock their egos into a fixed position, they jeopardize not only their enterprises, but also their careers. The simple fact is that no matter who we are, *our jobs are becoming obsolete.* The skill sets and habits that we call upon to do our work are a little less valuable every day.

"Never let your ego get so close to your position that when your position goes, your ego goes with it."

☑ *Let change lead growth*

---

*P*owell's career has been all about *change*. As noted before, changing things inevitably makes some people upset—even angry. Humans tend to resist change, even though it's change (which precipitates growth) that will keep them happily and gainfully employed. But the fact is that external change is *endemic*, *proliferating*, and *accelerating*. Therefore, leaders need to rewire perceptions, connecting these dots in more productive and positive ways.

In such a context, good leaders constantly prod their people with "what if?" and "why not?" questions. They engender a climate of a let's-try-it experimentation, demand innovation, and reward performance. They encourage a philosophy in which change becomes equivalent to growth and growth becomes equivalent to satisfaction.

Think about the pace of change that has prevailed in the last decade or so. Before the mid-1990s, few people were using e-mail, and few were even aware of something called the "World Wide Web." People did business by phone, fax, and FedEx. Then that world got turned upside down. As a new reality set in, a certain percentage of people simply chose to dig in their heels.

Savvy leaders realized that harnessing this change could lead to extraordinary growth and opportunity. Rather than waiting for the new reality to make their systems obsolete, a leader's role, in this situation, is to overcome institutional (and individual) inertia and let change lead growth.

One final point—change is not a one-shot deal. Change is a continuous, dynamic process that people must understand and embrace. The leader's job is to build a direction and foundation for sustained change, paving the way for continued growth and expansion in the organization. Here are some tactics to make change and growth part of your daily environment:

Encourage those around you to learn new skills: Create a climate in which people are valued for their ability to develop new skills and grab new responsibilities, thereby perpetually reinventing their jobs.

Replace the old missions with new ones: No organization can tolerate a vacuum in mission. If your old mission has become outdated, make sure that you define a new one and that everyone in your organization understands and supports the new goal.

Unlearn lessons—look beyond yesterday, and today: Don't let the organization stagnate. Even in the best of weather, look for competitive clues on the horizon. Adapt to new situations, and respond to them with innovative action.

"I'll bet you right now that there's no established organization where you won't find somebody who says ... I know what I've been doing for the last 15 years, and you're not going to screw me up."

☑ *Seek consensus (but don't be ruled by it)*

*P*owell is a team player, and he would be the first to say that the leader's role is to generate organizational consensus. How does that fit together with a willingness to piss some people off?

The answer lies in Powell's particular definition of "consensus" and how the leader should think about it. Emphatically, he does *not* equate consensus with "let's chew on this until we can all get happy"—a method Powell would see as an abdication of responsibility. Instead, Powell follows his own formula for achieving—and then using—consensus.

To begin with, he is *crystal clear* about the general direction in which he wants to steer the organization. After stating these expectations, Powell is aggressively inclusive. Everyone is invited—and expected—to participate in the new game. Having articulated his "simple standards" (his words) to State Department personnel shortly after taking the helm, he declared, "*I want everybody to be part of it.*" That's both an invitation and an expectation.

But clarity of purpose and inclusiveness only go so far toward building consensus. That's why Powell makes it his personal priority to *provide people with the necessary resources to successfully compete in the new game.* Concurrently, Powell works very hard to earn a personal commitment from every member of his team. He pushes no harder or faster than the emerging consensus will allow.

Even as Powell lays out his new agenda, he spends an enormous amount of time listening, learning, and involving people in the change process. He does this to make himself smarter and to help his employees better understand the why's and how's of change.

Don't assume, however, that Powell is prepared to wait patiently until everybody gets into line and declares himself or herself to be "ready for change." Let's face it: there are some people who will *never* come around and there are some circumstances that are too dire or desperate to allow for *any* sort of gradual process. In such cases, as we shall see in subsequent lessons, Powell is perfectly willing to throw himself out in front of the pack.

Here are three things you can do to make consensus building work for you:

Earn a personal commitment from every member of the team: Make sure that everyone is invited—and expected—to participate in the new game. When individuals become personally committed to the mission, the potential for success is greatly magnified.

Don't push harder or faster than the organization will allow: Change is a continuous, dynamic process that people must understand and accept. At times, giving people a little extra time to adjust to change can smooth ruffled feathers and, ultimately, protect the mission.

Seek consensus, but be prepared to move ahead decisively: There are some circumstances in which a gradual process is not an option. In these cases, a good leader will risk pissing people off for the good of the organization.

"Everyone wants me to reorganize, but I'm not reorganizing until I've got these folks on my side and believing in my leadership."

☐ Chase the trends

☑ *Fit no stereotypes*

---

*T*hroughout his career, Colin Powell has resisted chasing the latest trend or fad. At the same time, he also argues against falling into rigid patterns of behavior.

When a leader engages in "stereotypical behavior"—in other words, constantly leading people with a particular style or approach—it very often generates rigidity in thought and action. Powell has repeatedly told his staff, his interviewers, and his audiences that he can't be pegged and won't be stereotyped. He is wary of anyone—colleague or consultant—who promotes a "one best way" approach.

Powell also has little patience with buzzwords and catch phrases, such as "empowerment" and "power down." These are the phrases of *formula*—and, in most cases that involve humans in organizations, formulas don't apply. Some situations require the leader to hover closely; others require the timely appearance of long and loose leashes. Management techniques are not magic elixirs, but simply tools that wise leaders reach for at the right times, and then put back on the shelf.

Flexibility is all-important. On the other hand, Powell is not suggesting that leaders can operate in an "anything goes" philosophical vacuum. Nor is he suggesting that leadership can be boiled down to a completely opportunistic, value-free, "the ends justify the means" process. The opposite is true: the Powell Principles constitute a clear, strategic, philosophical, value-based, and ethical blueprint. The blueprint guides Powell, but the blueprint has enormous flexibility and opportunism built into it. If you get to the bridge and the bridge is out, you go look for another bridge—while still aiming for the same destination. Not sure if you're overly influenced by fads? Consider the following suggestions:

Be ready to change on a dime: No leader should plan on constantly shaking things up and shifting strategy. On the other hand, the best leaders run enterprises that are fleet and flexible.

Beware packaged solutions: Practical, action-oriented leaders think on their feet. They improvise. They understand that part of good leadership is the ability to employ the most effective tool for the situation at hand.

Don't limit your toolbox of management techniques: Management techniques are not magic elixirs, but simply tools that wise leaders reach for at the right times, and then put back on the shelf.

"Fit no stereotypes. Don't chase the latest management fads. The situation dictates which approach best accomplishes the team's mission. "

☐ **Complicate**

✓ *Simplify*

*A*nother imperative associated with Powell's lessons on mission and leadership is *simplify*. On a daily basis, cut through the morass of argument, debate, and doubt that sometimes accompanies mission-related debates. Offer solutions that are clear and understandable. The results? Strength of purpose, credibility of leadership, integrity in organization, and a consistent record of accomplishment.

Whether it's in the realm of values, policies, performance standards, or appropriate conduct, *keep it simple*. The world is chaotic, complicated, and murky. In that context, your personal laser beam (of principles, of commitment, of purpose) will help get your team home safely.

Effective leaders take the abstract and complex and render it into something that is graspable and straightforward. They articulate vivid, overarching goals and values, which they use to drive daily behaviors and make choices among competing alternatives. Their visions and priorities are lean and compelling. Even while they're tactically flexible, they convey an unwavering firmness and consistency in their actions, aligned with the picture of the future they are so carefully painting.

Part of the goal of simplicity is to generate a powerful internal consensus. "Consensus" has recently acquired a slightly negative connotation, signifying (to some people, at least) that a consensus-oriented organization is aiming for the lowest common denominator, and that the result will necessarily be tasteless and odorless.

This is unfair. Consider what a *lack* of consensus means for an organization. Can you really move toward a goal—*any* goal—if there's no agreement on that goal? And the harder the goal, the more commitment and tenacity your organization is going to need. Commitment and tenacity grow, in part, out of consensus. Here are three ways bring simplicity and clarity to your organization:

Define the game clearly, and expect everyone to play by it: Clearly articulate a broad agenda. Provide everyone with the tools and training necessary to take action. Insist that everyone take the responsibility to carve out the best ways to execute that agenda.

Make sure the mission reaches every part of the organization: Never stop articulating the message, up and down the hierarchy. When you are clear, consistent, and committed, you lend enormous strength to your organization.

Let overarching goals drive daily behavior: Consistency builds a leader's credibility and effectiveness. It's easier for the troops to follow you—literally and figuratively—if you say the same things every day and if these principles drive everything that the organization does.

"We had to make sure that we took the new mission and drove it down to the last private in the ranks. Whoever came in and emptied the trash can at night had to understand the vision."

☑ *Let situation dictate strategy*

*P*owell argues for a *situational* approach to leadership. In other words, he makes the case that effective leadership depends on a thorough immersion in the here and now—on a precise understanding of the situation at hand. Anything that clouds that vision or impedes effective action—be it an organizational rut, a stereotyped behavior, or the embrace of a succession of management fads—hurts the organization. The landscape changes; therefore, the effective leader is ever vigilant, ready to shift strategy and tactics as the situation warrants.

External conditions are always in flux (new competitors, new opportunities). Internal conditions continually change (new processes, new employees). And "when the environment changes," says Powell, "you have to change with it and try to get ahead of it."

"A foolish consistency," said Ralph Waldo Emerson, "is the hobgoblin of little minds." One size *never* fits all. This is true for management fads, which abound today in part because of the proliferation of business advisors and consultants. Flitting from fad to fad—even when those fads come dressed in sophisticated business jargon and embody some sensible principles—is very likely to damage the organization's ability to achieve its mission. Faddism generates confusion about priorities, reduces the leader's credibility, and drains organizational coffers and human resources. If the context changes dramatically, it is unlikely that your organization's established patterns of behavior will continue to be effective.

Generals, it is said, always fight the last war. That's understandable, especially when the last war led to glorious victory. But generals who think in the grooves of the last war are likely to be defeated. Each engagement is different. Each situation needs to be examined, and responded to, on its own merits.

Three tactics to consider in responding to the situation at hand are:

Avoid "one size fits all" solutions: There are no magic elixirs for every situation. A leader's job is to assess every situation and adopt a direction and a course of action that best fit the situation.

Be flexible: No leader should plan on constantly shaking things up and shifting strategy. On the other hand, the best leaders run enterprises that are fleet and flexible. Be prepared to change direction as the situation warrants it.

Don't fight "the last war": In times of uncertainty, don't assume "back to basics" is the right course of action. Many leaders fall into the trap of returning to the familiar when things get rough. Don't cling to stereotypical responses just because you're comfortable with them.

"Vague phrases such as 'power down' and 'centralized versus decentralized management' were not part of my vocabulary. I would give each of them whatever help was needed to get the job done."[1]

[1]Powell, Colin, with Joseph E. Persico, *My American Journey* (New York: Random House, 1995), pp. 319-320.

☑ *Push the envelope*

*C*olin Powell is methodical. He analyzes his circumstances and understands the rules of the game that he's playing. At the same time, however, he doesn't hesitate to push things to the limit when the situation warrants it. He doesn't hesitate to work *around* the rules of the game, creatively, without exactly breaking them. This is an important lesson—particularly in large organizations, in which bureaucracies all too often rule the day.

In most organizations above a certain level of complexity, if you ask for permission to do something new and interesting, you're very likely to wind up banging your head on a wall. You're almost certain to run into someone who will attempt to dilute or postpone your initiative. When people gain a secure position in what appears to be a safe and stable organization, they often feel that it's their job to *keep things exactly as they are.* Small wonder that organizational inertia is an epidemic and chronic disease!

To be sure, many organizations today are preaching the gospel of "empowerment" and "pushing authority down." But if you look behind the words, these supposedly aired-out hierarchies are seldom much more empowering than your average bureaucracy.

The best managers constantly skirt the edge, leaning out beyond their job descriptions and "official" responsibilities. They stretch the envelope, quite often without asking anybody's permission. They experiment, regularly trying new things out with their teams. Without being irresponsible or openly insubordinate, they bypass procedures and chains of command to get the job done.

What's stretching, pushing, being proactive, and dodging "no's" all about? Ultimately, it's all about *the individual spirit.* It's about what makes a job worth doing and—to some extent—what makes a life worth living. Here are some ways to be more proactive in your organization:

Don't look for "no's": Less effective middle managers tend to say, "If I haven't explicitly been told 'yes,' I can't do it." The best ones tend to say, "If I haven't explicitly been told 'no,' I *can* do it."

Live the old adage: "No guts, no glory": By taking calculated, intelligent risks, you are likely to accomplish more than playing it safe. It is easier to secure forgiveness than permission.

Don't punish for failure: As long as people are not subjecting your organization to undue risk, *it's never a sin to fail* when pursuing a good objective using sensible tools and tactics. Find ways to keep the organization from making the same mistake twice.

"You don't know what you can get away with until you try."

☐ Hedge your bets

☑ *Close with the enemy*

Powell tells us something critically important: *execution matters.* A plan is only as powerful as the *zeal to execute* upon which it's founded. Powell believes strongly that there is little sense even articulating a mission or laying out a battle plan unless you are prepared to pursue that mission and fight that battle with complete commitment. In other words, unless you're unequivocally committed to a path, don't even go there. This is why "close with the enemy" always comes first on his list. In wartime, it's what a soldier *must do.*

Does this mean that Powell is unconcerned about mission? Of course not. He believes *purpose must be inseparable from your commitment to achieving it.* An organization must know its "reason to exist." It must also know the possible end points, the tactics and weapons that are available to it, the competitive landscape, and so on. All of these help to drive mission definition and prepare you to pursue it with everything you've got. They are all part of an iterative loop. Mission drives plan; competitive reality sharpens and fuels mission.

This doesn't mean that a good leader can be inflexible—especially on the battlefield, where change and the unexpected are the only constants. Leaders need to tactically weave and bob in response to emerging events, even take a step sideways or back occasionally—provided, of course, they stay in relentless pursuit of their mission.

How do we bring this lesson home to a business context? Powell is telling us that we must *take on clearly defined battles that can be won—and won decisively.* Make sure that the goals are understood and endorsed by the people who need to endorse them. (And this ought to be a larger group, rather than a smaller group.) Finally, make it clear that these goals will be pursued with overwhelming strength. Here are three ways to incorporate the "close with the enemy" philosophy:

Execution is the key: Do not articulate a vision or a mission unless you are prepared to implement it with overwhelming strength. Stay cool under fire, think big, act fast, and go for the big win.

Pick your battles: Elevate to "mission status" only those causes that are vital to the organization's success.

Remain flexible: Pick your battles, but don't turn up your nose at opportunity. And even after you've settled on a winning strategy and tactics, be prepared to throw the game plan out the window in response to fast-moving circumstances.

"(Once) we have looked at all the rough edges and we have made a decision as to what we are going to do, then we are all going to move out in that decision and stick with it, with coherence and consistency over time, unless it has been proven that we should move in a different direction."

☐ View people as instruments

☑ View people as partners

*W*hen trying to get the most out of the people under his command, Powell adheres to two interrelated premises.

First, people are competent. As he once observed: "Officers have been trying for hundreds of years to outsmart soldiers and have still not learned that it cannot be done. We can always count on the native ingenuity of the American GI to save us from ourselves and to win wars." Powell regularly expresses his confidence in his people to solve their own problems, and to use their experience and expertise to help the organization attain its goals.

As an extension of this philosophy, Powell treats people as partners. When Powell describes his style as "collegial," he's going well beyond the surface attributes of accessibility, civility, and open-door listening. He's identifying a particular way that he treats people: not as "subordinates" who are expected to follow him blindly, but as partners who will bring their experience and expertise to the table and who will work *with* him to achieve exceptional goals.

Second, every task is important. In one of his early speeches to State Department staff, Powell proclaimed, "I also believe, to the depth of my heart, that there is no job in the State Department that is unimportant."

Many managers pay lip service to this philosophy, but don't live it. Powell lives it. Marshall Adair, president of the American Foreign Service Association, believes that it was Powell's military background that taught him that every task counts and that high morale is critical to getting the best out of people. That's why Powell goes out of his way to hammer home his message at every opportunity.

To some extent, Powell aims for the self-fulfilling prophecy. If you believe that your people are high-performers and if you convey that belief to them, they are likely to *be* high-performers. Consider the following suggestions for working with people in your organization:

Ignore hierarchy: Like most effective leaders, Powell sees every person as a partner who brings experience and expertise to help him achieve exceptional goals.

Depend on people, not plans... plans accomplish nothing: Without great people empowered by supportive cultures, the best-laid plans are likely to be of little use.

Spend at least 50% of your time on people: Surveys suggest that highly effective executives spend between 50% and 75% of their time on "people" issues.

"Our ability to successfully perform our mission depends, first and foremost, on the quality of our people .... We're all part of one quality family, working together as a family. No component more important than any other component."[1]

[1]Powell, Colin. From "Remarks at the Department of State Awards Ceremony," May 10, 2001. Washington, D.C. From the U.S. Department of State Web site, www.state.gov, visited 10/17/01.

☐ Pay deference to the pros

☑ *Challenge the pros*

---

*P*owell's advice on this subject is succinct and has profound implications for managers and professionals at every level: *"Don't be afraid to challenge the pros, even in their own backyard."* Those who want to have a significant impact on their organizations can't duck this responsibility.

Who are the "pros"? Simply put, they're people with authority and status. Most are inside the organization: your peers, your colleagues, your bosses, your boss's bosses, and so on. They run the place, wielding either formal or implicit power. But they may also be outside the organization—consultants, accountants, attorneys, or other providers of professional services. Or they made straddle some sort of divide, such as a major shareholder. The trait they all have in common is that they are able to wield significant power.

Some pros have earned their positions of power through exceptional performance, by acquiring and exercising vital skills. Others have earned their power position mainly by kissing up to the right people, skillfully expropriating the work of others, or simply by staying out of the way of trouble. I'd call these characters "phony pros," but their clout in many cases is no less real.

Because pros have clout, they can steer the enterprise in the right direction or, just as easily, down an errant path. They can make things happen or stop things from happening. They can raise spirits or depress them. They can affect people's performance, in either positive or negative ways. In extreme cases, they can put the organization, or people within, in danger.

When that happens, a good leader pushes back and challenges them. In fact, he believes that everyone in an organization has a positive *obligation* to pose this kind of challenge—not only peer-to-peer and down the ladder, but also up the ladder. This doesn't mean that an effective leader treats the pros disrespectfully. But the leader must also be fully prepared to assert that the pros can be wrong—that they can make ill-advised decisions, act inappropriately, or inadvertently give bad advice. Here are three ways to encourage challenges within your organization:

Tolerate rebels: If you're going to be speaking out, you need to be helping others speak out, too. It's the best way to get the best ideas on the table. Encourage those around you to challenge you and the other senior members of your team.

Emphasize respect while disagreeing: Disagree without being disagreeable. Powell challenges his bosses when necessary, but he does so in a way that respects the dignity of his superiors and preserves the dignity of his own position.

Challenge the pros to get to better solutions: Whether it's you challenging your superiors or your subordinates challenging you, remember that more opinions and more voices usually translates into more alternative options.

"Every organization should tolerate rebels who tell the emperor he has no clothes."

☑ *Don't rely on charts and titles*

*L*et's look at what Powell thinks *doesn't* work to enhance credibility and build authority. When Powell declares, "Organization charts and fancy titles count for next to nothing," he provides us with a broad clue. Focusing on the trappings of power—or on the fine shadings of an organization chart—is likely to interfere with the mission. At best, the organization stagnates; at worst, it goes off in a misguided direction.

An org chart is nothing more than a snapshot of an organization at a given point in time. It usually includes lots of small boxes containing the names of employees and their titles, with the boxes connected in ways that represent the relationships within the hierarchy.

But there's no way that an org chart can capture the dynamics of even the simplest human organizations. It's amazing how quickly an org chart becomes obsolete, even in the slowest-moving organization. So in many cases, smart employees learn to do the *right* thing, whether or not it appears in their job description or on a chart. Effective leaders learn how to encourage and harness this behavior. They teach their people to figure out how things actually work and get the job done based on this reality rather than on the snapshot.

As for the titles on that org chart, they may be linked to formal authority, but that doesn't mean they're linked to influence. Titles denote a certain level of prior performance, but they're no guarantee of future performance.

If you've ever worked in an organization, you've surely run across individuals who, despite fancy titles, don't seem to *get much done*. Conversely, you've probably also run across people who possess little formal authority, but who somehow get things done. They use some combination of pizzazz, drive, expertise, and a genuine commitment to something to get the organization to perform at a high level.

Leadership, says Powell, is less about authority and titles and more about *influence*. Managers invoke authority; leaders exert influence. Consider the following suggestions:

Respect authority, but don't be cowed by it: Paying undue attention to things like status and position won't get the job done.

Use charts as a guideline, but be ready to abandon them: Smart employees learn to ignore the org chart when necessary. And effective leaders tell their people to figure out how things actually work *today*, in this organization as it is currently populated and configured, and then get the job done.

Remember that titles are just titles: Titles don't necessarily translate into wisdom. Respect those in authority, but remember that leadership is about much more.

"Plans don't accomplish work. Goal charts on walls don't accomplish work .... It is people who get things done."

☐ Trust the inner circle

☑ *Trust those in the trenches*

*A*s our world moves more and more in the direction of complexity, unpredictability, and enormous changes at the last moment, smart leaders "cultivate a spirit of initiative and leadership among their smaller organizational units." They take the necessary steps to equip these smaller units with the tools and the authority they need to innovate. They decentralize, but they keep the clout and authority squarely behind the newly empowered subunits.

Why? Because when things are changing rapidly and the organizational vision is obscured, you have to count on your front-line troops. As Powell puts it, "The commander in the field is always right and the rear echelon is wrong, unless proven otherwise."

It's a quietly radical proposition, because it upends the traditional assumptions about power in an organization. And Powell clearly believes that this unorthodox approach applies to *all* organizations. As Secretary of State, Powell has asserted that "the real wisdom" lies with his ambassadors, rather than in the Washington bureaucracy. He says, unequivocally, "They're right out there, and we're wrong here until proven otherwise."

People in the trenches are closer to everything local—conditions, allies, enemies, customers, employees, suppliers, and competitors. They can make decisions and take actions that are faster, more informed, more flexible, and better fitted to local conditions. And this means that they'll make better, smarter, timelier, and more appropriate decisions.

Powell adds two qualifications to this message of decentralization. He's careful to state that his policy does not imply "open season" on the servants at the core: "If I find that any of you are dumping on my people without good cause, you can bet I'll come to their rescue."

A second caveat: Powell is *not* suggesting that top leadership is off the hook—before, during, or after decentralization. Top leadership is still responsible for ongoing oversight and accountable for organizational progress. Within this "loose-tight" framework, decentralization can work. Do you rely enough on the front line? Consider the following suggestions:

Take advantage of the intelligence of those in the field: Those not in touch with what is happening on the "front lines" can't make all the key decisions. If your division or unit is not decentralized, consider a deep, pervasive, structural, and cultural reorganization.

Use the Internet to ensure access to information: All members of the team must have access to key resources. Trusting those in the trenches means trusting them with information, and digital tools are a great help in leveling the knowledge playing field.

Stay involved and supportive: Decentralization is not an excuse for being out of touch. It is still the leader's responsibility to provide effective leadership. In times of crisis, strong leaders become much more involved—and their troops understand why they are doing so.

"The people in the field are closest to the problem, closest to the situation, therefore, that is where real wisdom is."

☑ *Make optimism a top priority*

*P*owell has made a simple and compelling observation—military in its specifics, but universally applicable—that forms the basis for this lesson: "Perpetual optimism is a force multiplier." By this, he means that a leader's enthusiasm, hopefulness, and confidence multiply as they radiate throughout the organization. Leaders who view the world positively and confidently tend to infuse their people with the same attitude.

The converse is also true: cynicism, doubt, and negativity can be "force shrinkers." In other words, leaders who persist in seeing the world negatively are very likely to demoralize, demotivate, and undermine the effectiveness of their colleagues.

Leaders don't have to smile through their tears or shrug off their frustrations. But the leader who begins and ends the day by saying things like *we can change things here, we can achieve awesome results*, or *we can be the best* is likely to bring a lot of people along with him or her. Optimism transforms doubters into believers. And sometimes, a good dose of optimism makes things possible that "realism" does not.

Optimists overestimate their skills and their capacity to influence events. Buoyed by their unrealistic view of the world, they show great resiliency in the face of adversity. As Winston Churchill once observed, "Success is measured by your ability to maintain enthusiasm between failures." Meanwhile, under more or less the same conditions, pessimists are giving up—same circumstances, diametrically opposite outcomes: the only difference is the outlook of the players.

There is also clear evidence that people resonate with positive messages. This impulse appears to reside somewhere deep in our human wiring. Most of the time, people will choose to follow a leader with an optimistic message rather than one with visions of doom and gloom. Powell understands and subscribes to the power of optimism.

Consider the following ways to incorporate optimism into your daily grind:

Spread optimism around the organization: The leader sets the tone, and he or she must be sure that optimism—not pessimism—permeates the fabric of the organization.

Don't take counsel of your fears or naysayers: Don't let naysayers or partial facts tell you that it can't be done. Remember—positive distortions of reality can be highly desirable.

Make optimism fuel for bold action: "Dynamic" optimists apply their optimism to attain goals and help others attain goals, as well. They take action. Don't just smile and shrug in the face of a problem—do something with the hand you've been dealt.

"Don't let adverse facts stand in the way of a good decision ... never step on enthusiasm."

☑ *Have fun in your command*

***P**owell advises us to *enjoy ourselves* and *have fun while we're working*. If you're not having fun, you're either in the wrong line of work or you're doing your job wrong.*

Successful leaders take their work and responsibilities *very seriously indeed*. You don't get to the top of a company, and then take that company to the top of its industry, without taking care of business. At the same time, successful leaders view fun in the workplace as essential to innovation, risk-taking, team spirit, and performance. When people have fun together, they are far more likely to accomplish extraordinary things together.

Enjoying each other begins with enjoying yourself. (This is a behavior that people are especially quick to imitate.) Enjoying yourself often begins with finding fun in the unexpected. It is sustained by humor, especially self-deprecating humor, and any other tools for puncturing stuffiness and pomposity.

One of the best predictors of a company's health is how much fun people are having as they are working their hardest. "Lots of fun" translates directly into "very healthy." Conversely, one of the best predictors of personnel turnover—and ultimately, corporate disease and demise—is when you start hearing the talented people say, "It's just not *fun* anymore." No matter how big the enterprise has become or how much momentum it seems to have, if there's no joy in the organization, all bets are off.

In today's fast-paced, fingernail-biting, competitive environment, a leader who doesn't have a sense of humor is unlikely to be effective over the long run. Leaders who want imagination, exuberance, and passion in the ranks need to inject the yeast of humor into their organizations. There's no one right style—in fact, imitating someone else's style is one of the surest paths to failure. But the leader needs to find *a* right style, for himself or herself and for the organization, and then work it.

Here are three ways to bring fun into your organization:

Work hard and play hard: In successful organizations, fun has emerged as a business priority and encouraging employees to "work hard and play hard" is an informal but powerful corporate value.

Create a fun environment for others: Fun can take the form of formal structures like on-site fitness centers, parties, and celebrations. But it should also be engrained in the work itself and in the working relationships.

Minimize unnecessary stress: Build realism into schedules and workloads. Identify sources of stress in the workplace and think about how they might be minimized. Conversely, identify sources of satisfaction and inspiration in the workplace and reinforce them.

"I told the ambassadors to take seriously their role as the President's personal representatives. At the same time, I encouraged them to have great fun in their new assignments. Fortunately, the two are not mutually exclusive."

☑ *Strive for balance*

What does balance have to do with leadership? We instinctively know what balance is—or, perhaps more accurately, what it isn't— because we've all seen *imbalanced* managers during our careers. There's the leader who is big on making sure everyone feels good, but keeps putting off the serious work. There's the manager who tenaciously defends the status quo. There's the intense workaholic who logs mind-numbing numbers of hours chained to her desk, but at the same time demonstrates little understanding of or empathy for her co-workers.

Today, Americans are working more and vacationing less. While this "living to work" philosophy has resulted in unparalleled wealth and productivity, it has also created extraordinary stresses and tensions in people's lives.

In fact, the "living to work/working to live" question (a question of balance) has become a major issue among managers and white-collar employees alike. It is likely to become an issue of worldwide importance, because an increasing number of countries around the world seem to be gravitating toward the American "living to work" model. Meanwhile, in the U.S., recent research suggests that employees are beginning to value time as much as money.

Leaders who do not buffer themselves and their people from the pressure to work constantly cannot remain effective in the long haul. "Do your work, and then go home to your families," Powell advises his subordinates. "Unless the mission demands it, I have no intention of being here on Saturday and Sunday. Do what you have to do to get the job done, but don't think that I am clocking anybody to see where you are on any particular hour of the day or day of the week."

Powell further advises leaders to extend this philosophy to those for whom they are responsible: "As a leader, you need to recognize that people need balance in their lives, have outside interests, have families and need to spend time with them. Unless absolutely unavoidable, you should not infringe on off-duty time."

How can you achieve balance? Here are some suggestions:

Take leave when you've earned it: Don't neglect home and family life. Don't spend yourself entirely at work. If your workplace gets jealous, think about a change.

Don't clock hours for hours' sake: Don't mistake activity with productivity. Get things done, take your vacations, and encourage others to do the same.

Don't always run at a breakneck pace: There may well be stretches of time when you're putting in 14 hours a day at the office or giving up weekends. But these have to be the exceptions to the balanced rule. No organization is sustainable that counts on burning up its people.

"Never become so consumed by your career that nothing is left that belongs only to you and your family. Don't allow your profession to become the whole of your existence."

☑ *Prepare to be lonely*

"**C**ommand is lonely," declares Powell. At the end of the day, after a leader has listened, collaborated, delegated, and empowered, it's time for him or her—nobody else—to make the decisive and critical decisions. It's time to set the right course of action, inspire hope and confidence, bless the right initiatives, anoint the right people, define the right standards, and define the right metrics. In other words, it's time to show true leadership. Your decisions may reflect input from many people, but they're *your* actions. And whatever the aftermath to those decisions, *you own it.*

Most people don't get enormous responsibility thrust upon them suddenly. Most leaders work their way up some kind of ladder, with increasing degrees of authority and responsibility along the way. At some point along that path, most aspiring leaders grapple with—or at least *ought* to grapple with—some very tough questions: Can I bear the final responsibility? Can I take the heat, when it comes? Can I stand alone?

The final responsibility for the success or failure of a mission rests with the leader. Real leaders *take* that responsibility, willingly and unquestionably. You can expect some very tough decisions to go along with the perks of high office, and you can expect to experience some deep anxiety when your decisions may put lives or organizations in peril.

Loneliness can't be avoided, but it should be offset. Clear communication is a vital tool. In times of crisis, the leader must paint an absolutely clear picture of what needs to happen. In effect, the leader is painting the picture that he or she will own, after the fact. The process of creating that picture not only clarifies the leader's thinking, but also reinforces his or her stature as a leader. When the time comes to celebrate victory—or own up to defeat—the organization is far more likely to close ranks behind the leader.

Here are some leadership tactics to consider:

Accept responsibility: Those who seek out responsibility have to be prepared to accept it. Failures are their own; successes belong to their colleagues.

Lead by example: All employees are boss-watchers. The rank and file will always take their cues from the leader. It is therefore doubly important that the leader live the values he or she espouses.

Know when to exit: When you've figured it all out, it's time to pass it along to the next generation. Sometimes leaving is the greatest act of leadership.

"Sitting alone in the dark in the back seat of my car, I felt full of foreboding. I was going to be involved in conducting a war, one that I had urged, one that was sure to spill blood. Had I been right? Had my advice been sound?"

"Sometimes I think that I'm probably sounding a little too ... preachy. But then I realize that all I'm talking about are values, values I was raised with, that you were probably raised with, that are traditional American values .... Even if it's corny, it's still valuable."

_____

"If you are going to achieve excellence in big things, you develop the habit in little things. Excellence is not an exception, it is a prevailing attitude"

_____

Other Titles in the McGraw-Hill Professional Education Series

The Welch Way: 24 Lessons from the World's Greatest CEO
    by Jeffrey A. Krames (0-07-138750-1)

    Quickly learn some of Jack Welch's winning management practices in 24
    basic lessons. A great way to introduce yourself and your employees to the
    principles that made Jack Welch one of the most successful CEOs ever.

The Lombardi Rules: 26 Lessons from Vince Lombardi—the World's Greatest Coach
    by Vince Lombardi, Jr. (0-07-141108-9)

    A quick course on the rules of leadership behind Coach Vince Lombardi
    and how anyone can use them to achieve extraordinary results.

How to Motivate Every Employee: 24 Proven Tactics to Spark Productivity
in the Workplace
    by Anne Bruce (0-07-141333-2)

    By a master motivator and speaker, quickly reviews practical ways you can
    turn on employees and enhance their performance and your own.

The New Manager's Handbook: 24 Lessons for Mastering Your New Role
    by Morey Stettner (0-07-141334-0)

    By the author of the best-selling title on the same subject from the Briefcase
    Books series, here are 24 quick and practical practices to help new managers
    succeed.

The Powell Principles
Order Form

1–99 copies	_____ copies @ $7.95 per book
100–499 copies	_____ copies @ $7.75 per book
500–999 copies	_____ copies @ $7.50 per book
1,000–2,499 copies	_____ copies @ $7.25 per book
2,500–4,999 copies	_____ copies @ $7.00 per book
5,000–9,999 copies	_____ copies @ $6.50 per book
10,000 or more copies	_____ copies @ $6.00 per book

Name _____

Title _____

Organization _____

Phone (_____)_____

Street address _____

City/State (Country) _____ Zip _____

Fax (_____)_____

Purchase order number (if applicable) _____

Applicable sales tax, shipping and handling will be added.

☐ VISA ☐ MasterCard ☐ American Express

Account number _____ Exp. date _____

Signature _____

Or call 1-800-842-3075
Corporate, Industry, & Government Sales

The McGraw-Hill Companies, Inc.
2 Penn Plaza
New York, NY 10121